eyew⊙nder
Rocks and Minerals

THIRD EDITION
Senior Editor Rupa Rao
Senior Art Editor Ragini Rawat
US Editor Heather Wilcox
US Senior Editor Shannon Beatty
US Executive Editor Lori Cates Hand
Picture Researcher Ridhima Sikka
Deputy Manager, Picture Research Virien Chopra
Managing Editors Gemma Farr, Kingshuk Ghoshal
Managing Art Editors Govind Mittal, Elle Ward
DTP Designer Ashok Kumar
Production Editor Vishal Bhatia
Production Controller Joss Moore
Jacket Designer Vidushi Chaudhry
DK Delhi Creative Head Malavika Talukder
Art Director Mabel Chan
Managing Director Sarah Larter

Consultant Douglas Palmer

FIRST EDITION
Written and edited by Caroline Bingham
Publishing Manager Susan Leonard
Consultant Kim Dennis-Bryan PhD, FZS

This American edition, 2025
First American Edition, 2003
Published in the United States by DK Publishing,
a division of Penguin Random House LLC
1745 Broadway, 20th Floor, New York, NY 10019

Copyright © 2003, 2014, 2025 Dorling Kindersley Limited
25 26 27 28 29 10 9 8 7 6 5 4 3 2 1
001–348658–May/2025

All rights reserved.
Without limiting the rights under the copyright reserved above, no part of this publication may be reproduced, stored in or introduced into a retrieval system, or transmitted, in any form, or by any means (electronic, mechanical, photocopying, recording, or otherwise), without the prior written permission of the copyright owner.

Published in Great Britain by Dorling Kindersley Limited
A catalog record for this book is available from the
Library of Congress.
ISBN 978-0-5939-6750-8

DK books are available at special discounts when for sales promotions, premiums, fund-raising, or educational use. For details, contact: DK Publishing Special Markets, 1745 Broadway, 20th Floor, New York, NY 10019
SpecialSales@dk.com

Printed and bound in China

www.dk.com

Contents

4–5
Rocky Earth

6–7
A volcanic beginning

8–9
Making of a rock

10–11
Igneous rock

12–13
Sedimentary rock

14–15
Metamorphic rock

16–17
Rocks from space

18–19
Hidden beauty

20–21
Breakdown

22–23
Carving a path

24–25
Crystals

26–27
What a gem!

28–29
Precious metals

30–31
Get that metal!

32–33
Rocks in art

34–35
Using rocks

36–37
Building rocks

38–39
A touch of mystery

40–41
History in a rock

42–43
Hunting for rocks

44–45
What does it make?

46–47
What's this?

48–49
A safe path

50–51
Facts match

52–53
Hunt that treasure!

54–55
Glossary

56
Index and Acknowledgments

Rocky Earth

Rocks and minerals make up much of our planet and are mined to provide many of the things around us, from cars to computers. Even your body contains minerals that keep you alive.

Atmosphere

Like an onion
Earth is made up of layers, like an onion! It has a solid inner core at the center of the planet, surrounded by a molten outer core. Around this is a mantle of hot semiliquid rocks, and then the thin solid crust.

Fast facts

Your body contains more than 60 minerals. Out of these, 13 are essential for life.

Some minerals take thousands of years to form. Some form in minutes.

Oceans cover more than 70 percent of the planet's surface.

Earth's crust is between 3 and 50 miles (5 and 80 km) thick.

Earthly goods
Everything we use in our everyday lives is made of materials that come from our planet.

Jewelry

Computer

Cell phone

Crayon

Mantle
Outer core
Inner core

Ball of rock
Our rocky world formed around 4.5 billion years ago. This ancient planet was hot and molten. It took 500 million years to cool down and become a ball of rocks and minerals.

Let's make a rock
Most rocks are made up of mineral crystals. Different amounts of minerals make up different rocks (though some rocks are made from just one mineral).

Feldspar (pink and white)
Mica (black)
Quartz (grey)

quartz crystals + feldspar crystals + mica crystals = granite (a type of rock)

Car Clothes House

A volcanic beginning

Shake a bottle of fizzy drink and unscrew the cap. The bubbly overflow is a little like what happens when a volcano erupts. Whoosh! Out fly rocks, ash, dust, and gases!

Mega eruptions
A volcanic eruption may be powerful enough to destroy parts of the volcano. One of the sides of the Indonesian volcano Anak Krakatau (above) collapsed when it erupted in 2018.

No place for a rock?
Deep under Earth's crust, it is hot enough to melt rock. This molten rock is called magma. It can build up in chambers and burst through weak spots in Earth's crust.

Solid remains from previous eruptions build up a cone-shaped exterior.

Hot, light magma rises up inside the volcano.

Magma (molten rock) chamber

Shiprock Pinnacle is named after a ship, as it looks a little like one.

Ancient relic
Shiprock Pinnacle in New Mexico is all that remains of an ancient volcano—its solidified neck.

Broken volcanic rock filled the central vent of the volcano over time to form this structure.

Volcanic dust

Volcanic gravel

Volcanic rock

Many layers
The eruption of a volcano can create deep layers of ash, dust, and rock at its base, as seen in Santorini Island, Greece.

Volcanic debris ranges from dust and ash to rocks the size of houses.

Making of a rock

Do you think that all rocks look the same? In fact, there are hundreds of different kinds of rocks, but they can be divided into three basic types, which are being formed (and destroyed) as you read this book.

Cliffs showing layers of sedimentary rock

Getting hotter

Metamorphic rock forms when rocks are transformed as a result of being squeezed and heated deep under Earth's crust.

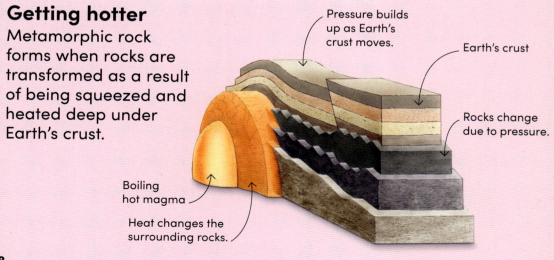

Pressure builds up as Earth's crust moves.

Earth's crust

Rocks change due to pressure.

Boiling hot magma

Heat changes the surrounding rocks.

In the beginning
Earth's first rocks were igneous rocks. These form from molten rock that has cooled and hardened.

Igneous rock formed from cooling lava

Chipping away
One way sedimentary rock forms is when sediments carried by wind and water build up in huge piles in rivers and seas. Over thousands of years, some of these become towering seaside cliffs of layered sedimentary rock.

Sediments settle at the bottom of lakes, rivers, and seas.

Sedimentary rock builds up in layers.

Sediments are squashed together.

Cliff showing the metamorphic rock called slate

From hair to glass
A volcano produces a great variety of igneous rocks. Just take a look at the three examples shown below.

Pumice is very light, bubble-filled volcanic lava.

Pele's hair looks like hair! It forms from sprays of lava.

Obsidian has a shiny surface because it is a volcanic glass.

Pumice stones have thousands of tiny holes in them.

Igneous rock

Much of Earth's crust is made of igneous rocks, which form from magma. A famous igneous rock formation is the Devils Tower National Monument in Wyoming.

Fast facts

"Igneous" comes from the Latin word for "fire."

When molten rock erupts from deep inside the crust, it becomes lava.

The more slowly that a rock cools from its molten form, the larger the crystals.

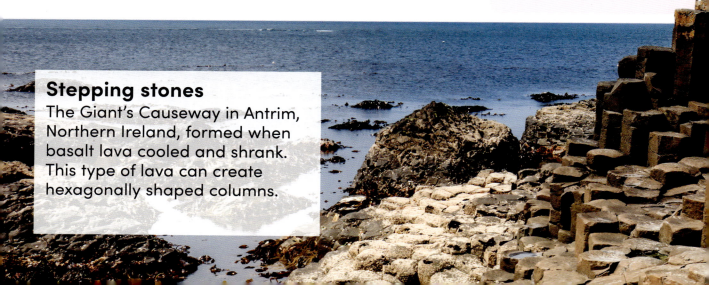

Stepping stones
The Giant's Causeway in Antrim, Northern Ireland, formed when basalt lava cooled and shrank. This type of lava can create hexagonally shaped columns.

👁 BUILT TO LAST

The most common igneous rock on land is granite. It is incredibly strong and has been used for building for thousands of years. The 11th-century Brihadeeswara Temple in southern India is made of granite.

Such minerals as mica and quartz make granite look speckled.

Legends say giants used the causeway as stepping-stones.

One by one
Remains of tiny sea creatures form these layers of chalk. It is thought that these layers in the Møns Klint cliffs in Denmark grew by 0.02 in (0.5 mm) a year—that's about 180 of these creatures piled on top of one another.

In places, these cliffs are 300 ft (90 m) high.

Sedimentary rock

Towering cliffs of chalk limestone are an amazing example of sedimentary rock. They are formed from the remains of the chalky, calcium-rich shells of tiny sea creatures.

Forming coal
As plants are buried, they are squeezed together, eventually forming the sedimentary rock called coal.

Year 1...

From plant matter...

at hundreds of years...

to peat...

Sandstone
The yellowish color comes from iron minerals in the rock.

Let's play
Do you like to play in golden sand? This is a sediment. Left for millions of years, it may eventually form sandstone, a sedimentary rock.

Such minerals as silica or iron oxide hold the pebbles together.

Chalk takes millions of years to form.

All mixed together
This sedimentary rock formed when pebbles stuck together, like a cake mix.

at millions of years...   **and after tens of million of years...**

to lignite...

to bituminous coal...

... to hard coal

13

Metamorphic rock

"Metamorphic" comes from the ancient Greek words *meta* (meaning "change") and *morphe* (meaning "form"). When rocks are heated and compressed inside Earth's crust, this type of rock forms.

The oldest-known metamorphic rock on Earth is around 4 billion years old.

Ice-cream swirls
When rocks are pressed and heated, the minerals inside them start to melt and squeeze into surrounding rocks. This makes a swirly patterned metamorphic rock called migmatite.

From magma
Deep under Earth's surface, heat melts rocks into a liquid called magma. When this magma touches such rocks as limestone, it changes the limestone to a metamorphic rock called lapis lazuli (left).

The bright blue color in lapis lazuli comes from a mineral called lazurite.

A peek at slate
The metamorphic rock slate starts as mud, which becomes compressed into a rock called shale. Then, this is squeezed into slate.

Mining marble
The metamorphic rock marble is mined by being cut into huge blocks with strong cutting wires.

👁 MARBLE MAGIC

Marble is formed from the sedimentary rock limestone. Polished marble looks stunning when used for buildings or carved into statues. Italian artist Michelangelo carved the famous sculpture *David* (right) out of a single block of white marble. Other stunning structures made of marble include the Taj Mahal in India.

Rocks from space

We cannot see it, but more than 9.8 tons of dust rain down on Earth every day. Most of the dust and rocks from space burn up in the atmosphere. Sometimes, a large rock crashes into Earth's surface. This is called a meteorite.

I spy a shooting star
Small space rocks, called meteors (shooting stars), can be seen as they burn up in Earth's atmosphere, usually more than 50 miles (80 km) above our heads.

Where do they come from?
Meteorites may have broken off asteroids, large chunks of rock that orbit the sun, mainly between Mars and Jupiter.

What's inside?
Meteorites from asteroids contain such metals as iron as well as rocks. Those from comets contain more rock than metal.

A large meteorite hit Earth 66 million years ago!

What's that hole?

If a large meteorite hits Earth, it can form a crater, changing the surroundings where it lands. It would take you about 30 minutes to walk across this meteorite crater in Australia.

This crater is old enough for trees to have grown in its base.

Just passing

Comets are a bit like huge snowballs, but made of ice, gases, and dust. They orbit the sun, developing long tails as they near it.

ONCE IN A LIFETIME

Halley's comet

One of the most famous comets, Halley's, was included in an embroidered artwork called the Bayeux Tapestry, stitched more than 900 years ago. Halley's comet passes Earth just once every 76 years. It last passed us in 1986.

A comet's tail can be 62 million miles (100 million km) long.

Hidden beauty

Brrrr! A cave is a damp, dark, chilly place. However, if you are lucky enough to visit a large cave that has been lit and opened to visitors, you'll discover incredibly beautiful shapes in the rocks.

Stalactites hang down, while stalagmites grow upward.

Carving caves
Over time, the flow of water eats away at solid rock. Water can dissolve the calcium carbonate (calcite) minerals that make the sedimentary rock limestone. Cracks in rocks widen to become fissures, passages, and then caves, such as this one in Grahovo, Slovenia.

Taking the time
Rock formations in caves build up drip by drip. It can take 1,000 years for them to grow less than a centimeter.

The tallest stalagmite in the world is the height of a 16-story building.

Build it up
The slender shapes in this cave built up gradually as drops of water evaporated, leaving deposits of the mineral called calcite.

Lava cave
As hot, molten lava flows, its surface cools faster and hardens, forming a "ceiling." When the lava has flowed out, the empty space below the ceiling becomes a lava cave.

Breakdown

Rocks are not as permanent as you may think. From driving rain to crashing waves, when rocks are exposed to wind, water, glaciers, or shifts in temperature, changes begin to happen.

If a hoodoo loses its protective cap, the structure will soon begin to wear away.

Attack by sea
A long time ago, these stacks were a part of Australia's coastline, but they have been cut off from the coast after constant battering from the sea.

The layers that make up the sedimentary rock can be seen clearly.

Attack by wind and water
Hoodoos, such as these in Alberta, Canada, are columns of soft sandstone topped by harder rock caps. The cap has protected the rock beneath it from being washed away by heavy rain.

Attack by river
Over millions of years, the Colorado River has carved its way down into the Grand Canyon, exposing rock layers 6,000 ft (1,829 m) deep.

Attack by acid rain
Pollution from factories and vehicles attacks rock. The gases in rainwater can make acids that eat into rock—as seen on some damaged statues.

Hoodoos form spectacular shapes, all clustered together.

Fast facts

The wearing away of a landscape is known as erosion.

Plants add to rock erosion as their roots burrow their way into cracks in rocks.

When rocks are broken down where they stand, it is known as weathering.

Slow progress
Glaciers usually creep just a few centimeters a day. They end lower down the mountain, where the ice melts away, or at the coast, where large blocks called icebergs break off.

Reid Glacier, Alaska

A glacier carves a deep valley as it moves forward.

The force of a glacier is enough to crumble rock.

Carving a path

When layers of snow pile up on a mountain, the lowest layers become ice. The weight of the snow forces the ice to flow, picking up rocks as it moves. This huge, slow-moving mass is a glacier.

👁 CLIMATE CHANGE

A rise in our planet's temperatures because of climate change is causing glaciers to melt faster. The Franz Josef Glacier in New Zealand has retreated more than 0.6 mile (1 km) since 2008. Its snow cover is still melting today.

2008

2022

From rock to flour!
Rocks carried by glaciers grind the walls of the glacial valley. The scratching produces fine grains of rock, known as rock flour.

Scratches and scrapes left by moving glacial ice

Rock flour is carried on down the glacier. Some is deposited in mountain lakes.

Sprinkle on the color!
Mountain lakes are often incredible shades of turquoise blue. This is because of the rock flour fed into them by a melting glacier.

23

Crystals

Have you ever cut out a paper snowflake? Snowflakes are made from tiny ice crystals that collide and stick together. Some types of crystals also form in rock and can be cut and polished.

Aquamarine crystal

Beautiful colors
Many crystals come in a rich range of colors. This pale blue aquamarine is a form of the mineral beryl.

From little to big
The tiny grains that form sand are usually made of quartz, which can grow into gigantic crystals. The largest cluster of crystals ever found weighed more than 14 tons!

Rose quartz crystals

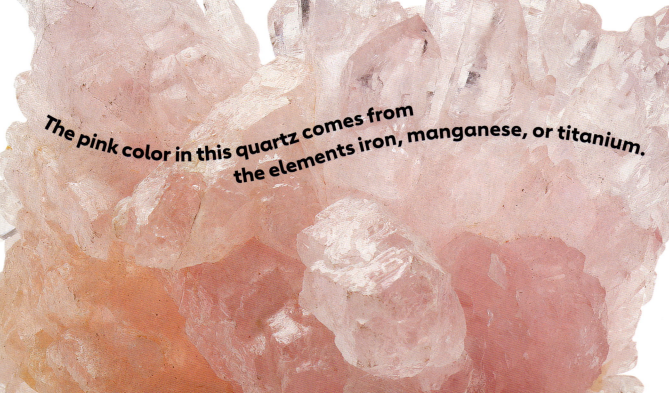

The pink color in this quartz comes from the elements iron, manganese, or titanium.

Is it a crystal?
Not all crystals look the same. The crystals of the mineral asbestos look like silky white threads—but they are dangerous and should not be touched!

Salt plains
Salt may not seem like a rock, but it is a crystalline rock. Salt plains, such as this one in Bolivia, are covered by a thick layer of salt.

Salt crystals form when seawater evaporates.

👁 A SALTY STAY

In Bolivia, there are hotels built from salt bricks, including the ceiling, walls, chairs, and tables. The buildings face some damage during the rainy season, and licking the salt is definitely not allowed!

The power to heal?
Some people believe that certain minerals have special powers. Jade is thought to help relaxation.

Jade carved into the shape of a dragon

What a gem!

From sparkling diamonds to rich red rubies, some minerals are valuable and are known as gems. They are often rare and colorful. Gems can be cut and polished and worked into jewelry.

Not just a rock

Most gemstones come from rocks. Imagine that you were lucky enough to find these rocks with green emeralds and blue sapphires!

Emerald in rock

Sapphire in rock

Rubies of the highest quality are found in marble.

Rubies get their red color from a metal called chromium.

Which one is yours?

Do you know your birthstone? Some people believe that it is lucky to wear a gem linked to their month of birth.

January	February	March	April	May
Garnet	Amethyst	Aquamarine	Diamond	Emerald

Diamond is the hardest mineral of all.

Diamonds come in more than 10 colors, but the purest ones are white.

Shine on
A cut stone reflects more light, just like this diamond. A cut diamond may have as many as 70 flat sides.

Pearl forms in certain shellfish, especially oysters.

Amber is the fossilized resin of some pine trees. It sometimes contains trapped insects.

Jet is the fossilized remains of wood.

Are all gems rocks?
Most gems form in rocks, but there are some gems, such as pearl, amber, and jet, that don't form in rocks. These are softer than most gems and are usually polished, not cut.

June	July	August	September	October	November	December

Pearl	Ruby	Peridot	Sapphire	Opal	Topaz	Turquoise

Precious metals

Gems are not the only treasures hidden deep within our rocky planet. Precious metals, such as gold, silver, and platinum, have long been mined and used to make objects of great beauty.

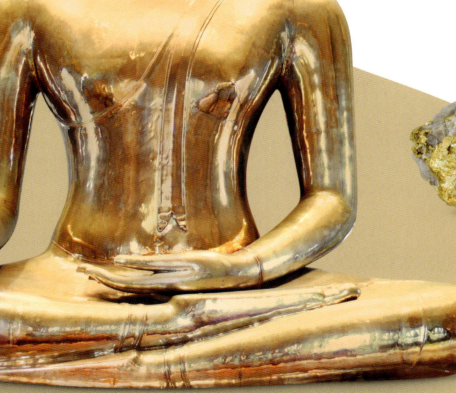

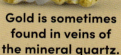

Gold is sometimes found in veins of the mineral quartz.

Gold
Bangkok, in Thailand, is home to the Golden Buddha, a statue made of solid gold. It weighs 6.1 tons—the weight of a small truck.

Silver

This soft metal was once used to make coins, jewelry, and figurines. The Inca people, who lived in what is now Peru, made this llama figurine.

Silver coins from ancient Egypt

Raw silver is often mined as nuggets.

The silver in this figurine is mixed with some copper and gold to make it stronger.

This platinum nugget weighs 2.4 lb (1.1 kg), around the same as 10 apples.

Platinum

One of the most expensive metals today is platinum. No wonder it was used to make this crown, part of the British Crown Jewels.

Let's make a hole
Most metals are collected from open-cast mines, such as this copper mine in Peru. Its surface is blasted, and tons of rock are removed by the truckload.

An open-cast mine has a network of roads to move the ore.

Get that metal!

Some metals are held inside rocks as minerals—the rock that holds the mineral is known as the ore. Some ores are near the surface, and some are deep underground.

Deadly damage
Mining harms the environment and the health of the people who work in these mines. An open-cast mine is also a noisy place.

👁 USING COPPER

Copper conducts electricity well and doesn't rust easily. This makes it a good choice for many electrical goods, including wires, coils for transformers on a circuit board (right), and even motors for electric cars.

Copper ore

A green film forms on copper when it reacts with air.

Tin ore

The first bronze statue may have been made in 2500 BCE.

Mixing metals

Metals are often melted down and joined to other metals to make a stronger material called an alloy. Copper and tin are mixed to produce the alloy bronze.

Bronze casts are made by pouring molten bronze into a mold. It then sets.

31

Rocks in art

Have you ever used a rock to draw? It's great fun to use chalk and scribble away on a sidewalk. The colors held inside some rocks and minerals have been used by artists for thousands of years.

The Chauvet Cave in France has more than 1,000 cave paintings.

Who needs paper?
Cave painters had no paper, so they used rock as their canvas. They mixed materials to produce just four or five colors.

Cave painters made the color black by using charcoal—the remains of burned wood and bone.

Fast facts

Clay was often used by early artists as a coloring for green and brown.

For thousands of years, people crushed colored rocks and mixed the powder with animal fat to make paints.

Rich reds
The powder of a toxic mineral called cinnabar makes a brilliant red. This was widely used in European religious art in the Middle Ages.

Cinnabar's color can range from red-orange to dark maroon.

Chalk was used to make the first white coloring for art.

Chalk can lighten a sketch.

A light source
The sedimentary rock chalk is messy to use, but it can help show how light bounces off an object.

33

Using rocks

A long time ago, somebody somewhere picked up a stone and used it as a tool. Over time, people found more and more ways in which to use rocks.

Taking shape
Flint can be shaped by chipping at it with another stone. That's how this prehistoric spearhead (left) and arrowhead (above) were made.

The granite used in Machu Picchu is believed to have formed 250 million years ago.

Stone city
The 15th-century city of Machu Picchu (in what is now Peru) was built out of stone by the Inca people. Its massive granite stones were cut precisely to fit each other and protect the buildings from earthquakes.

Flint scraper
Flint has sharp edges and was widely used in prehistory. The first flint tools, such as this fur scraper, were basic—but did the job.

A sharp, angled edge was used to soften an animal's hide.

Fast facts
Rocks have been used for many things, including weapons, tools, containers, and statues.

Hand axes, which had no handles, were first used more than 1.76 million years ago.

Let's make flour
Grain was first ground to make flour in this way some 6,000 years ago. Rocks like these were an early way of crushing the grain, but they made a coarse flour.

A smaller stone was used to grind the grain placed on the larger, flat stone.

A helpful handle
Hand-held rocks were gradually combined with handles to make axes. This stone was held in a length of wood by a tightly bound length of twine.

The handle has been remade—the original rotted away long ago.

Building rocks

Rocks are the building blocks of modern cities. Materials made of rocks are everywhere—in the roads, in the houses in which we live, and in the skyscrapers that tower above us.

Brick by brick
Bricks are made from clay, which is shaped in molds and fired in huge ovens, called kilns, to bake it.

Skyscrapers
Many types of artificial materials are put on a steel frame to make a skyscraper. Some of these come from rocks that have been mined.

A building has to be at least 492 ft (150 m) tall to be called a skyscraper.

Rock solid

Mix these ingredients, and you will make concrete, a building material that quickly sets rock-hard. It is used all over the world.

sand + gravel + cement + water = concrete

The building's steel framework is strong, but also flexible in high winds.

Glassy things

Natural glass forms when lava cools. The first glass objects were beads made about 3,600 years ago.

Shanghai, China

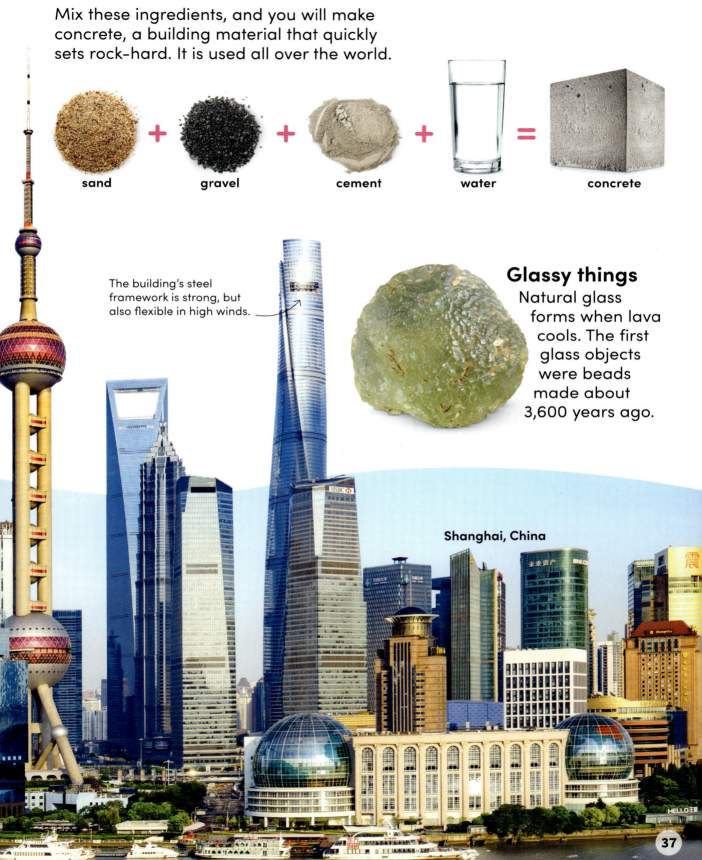

A touch of mystery

Some rocks and minerals look so unusual that myths and legends have grown up around them. From Devil's toenails to desert roses, the weird and wonderful are all around us.

Surf's up

Wave Rock in Australia is well named. This curved wall made of granite looks like a giant wave. Weathering makes its lower levels crumble away more easily than its upper lip.

The streaks are caused by minerals being washed down the rock by downpours of rain.

Magnetic charm
Magnetite is an iron mineral, which can become magnetic when struck by lightning. Here, it attracts iron filings and a metal paper clip.

Odd fossils
These rocks were once believed to be the Devil's toenails. In fact, they are fossils—the shells of extinct oysters.

Fake roses
Desert roses may look pretty, but they have no smell. They form from minerals, such as barite (left).

Made of lightning
It may look like a tree root, but this is fulgurite. This mineral forms when lightning strikes sand and fuses the grains.

Wave Rock is the height of a three-story house.

👁 A HISSING STONE?
Snakestones were once believed to be the remains of coiled snakes turned to stone by a 7th-century abbess named St. Hilda. They are actually the fossil shells of extinct sea creatures called ammonites on which snakelike heads have been carved.

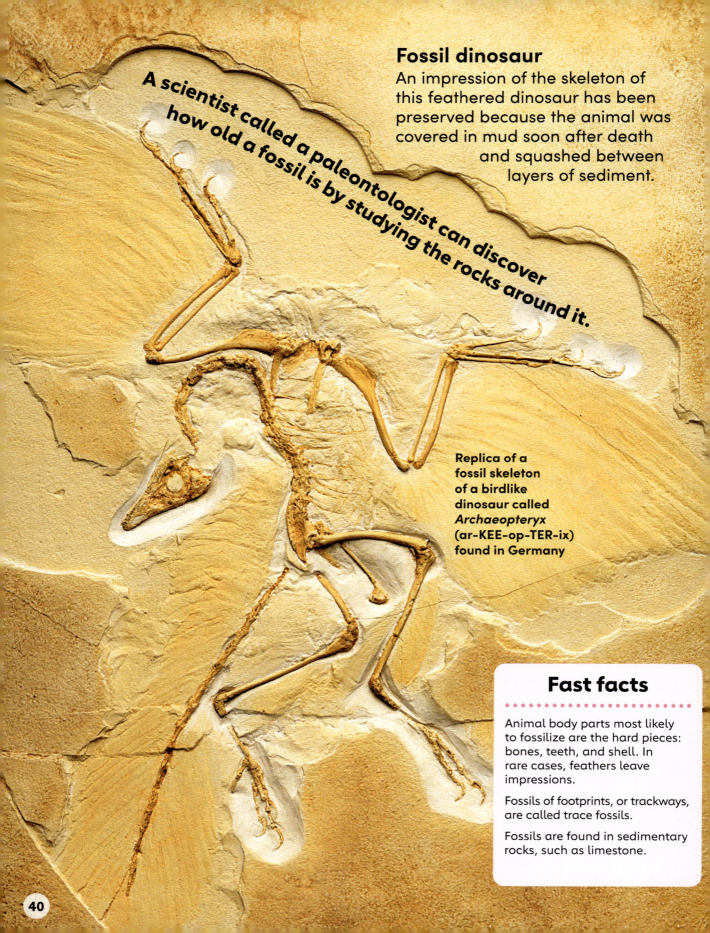

Fossil dinosaur

An impression of the skeleton of this feathered dinosaur has been preserved because the animal was covered in mud soon after death and squashed between layers of sediment.

A scientist called a paleontologist can discover how old a fossil is by studying the rocks around it.

Replica of a fossil skeleton of a birdlike dinosaur called *Archaeopteryx* (ar–KEE–op–TER–ix) found in Germany

Fast facts

Animal body parts most likely to fossilize are the hard pieces: bones, teeth, and shell. In rare cases, feathers leave impressions.

Fossils of footprints, or trackways, are called trace fossils.

Fossils are found in sedimentary rocks, such as limestone.

History in a rock

Rocks hide a lot of things, but perhaps the most exciting are the secrets rocks tell about life on Earth millions of years ago, when the dinosaurs ruled.

Clean-up time
It takes a long time to extract a large fossil from the rock in which it is encased. The paleontologist working on it does not want to damage it.

The rock and dust surrounding a fossil are removed particle by particle, if necessary.

Old gnashers
Teeth are commonly found fossils—they last well because they are so hard. This tooth belonged to a dinosaur called *Tyrannosaurus rex* (TIE-ran-oh-SORE-us reks).

What's that?
Imagine your footsteps being found by somebody in the future, preserved forever in rock. Fossil footprints, such as this dinosaur imprint in Spain, are a curious reminder of creatures long dead.

A tooth of a *Tyrannosaurus rex* could be as long as 12 in (30 cm).

Tyrannosaurus rex

Hunting for rocks

Once you begin to learn about rocks and minerals, it's fun to go look for some interesting rocks yourself. You may find a rock containing a fossil!

Ammonites were ancient marine creatures similar to a squid or octopus.

Just like today
Some fossils resemble animals that are alive today. This section of a nautilus shell (above) shows chambers similar to those seen in ancient ammonites.

Mohs scale
Geologists use Mohs scale, which was set up in 1812, to measure a rock's hardness against 10 known minerals. A number on the scale means that the rock can be scratched by minerals with the numbers above it.

1 Talc **2** Gypsum **2.5** Fingernail **3** Calcite **4** Fluorite

The nautilus builds its shell from calcium carbonate.

Fossil hunter
Collecting rocks and fossils is fun. But be careful when looking for them—stay away from cliffs, watch out for waves, and beware of dangerous creatures that may lurk under rocks!

Start your collection by hunting for fossils on the beach.

Coelacanth

Coelacanth fossil

Fossil or not?
"Living fossils" are creatures that were known as fossils before they were found to be still living. An example is a fish called a coelacanth.

Surprise inside!
From the outside, an amethyst rock looks a little bit dull. But hiding inside is a beautiful mass of shiny crystals.

5.5 Steel nail

5 Apatite

6 Orthoclase

7 Quartz

8 Topaz

9 Corundum

10 Diamond

What does it make?

Rocks and minerals, and the metals that are taken from them, can be found in many of the everyday objects that surround you. Just take a look!

Clay is used in... books, pencils, pottery

Fluorite is used in... ceramics, water, toothpaste

Garnet is used in... sandpaper, glass, jewelry

Limestone is used in... cleaning products, books, concrete

What's this?

Here are some remarkable rocks and minerals—and your challenge is to identify them. Look at the pictures and read the clues to see whether you can figure out what they are. Good luck!

1 This is fossilized tree resin. Millions of years ago, an insect became trapped inside it.

2 This is a giant, human-made hole in the surface of Earth.

It has a network of roads to transport ores.

3 This creature's shell is made of calcium carbonate.

Its shape is very similar to some ancient fossils.

4 This entire building is made of a crystalline rock we eat every day.

But licking its walls is not allowed!

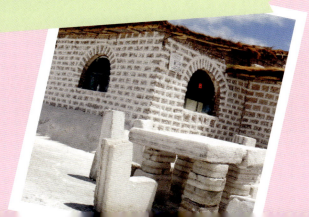

5 This precious blue gem is found inside rocks.

It can be cut and polished to make beautiful jewelry.

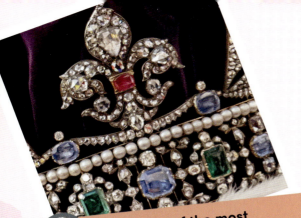

7 This ancient cave has more than 1,000 paintings.

The painters used charcoal to make black drawings on its walls.

6 This is one of the most expensive metals today.

It has been used to make this crown, which is a part of the British Crown Jewels.

9 This crystal is thought to have healing powers.

It may help with relaxation!

8 These are large, hexagonal columns.

They formed when hot, molten lava cooled and then shrank as it solidified.

10 This sandy mineral forms a roselike shape.

It is abundant in deserts.

11 This light stone is made of bubble-filled volcanic lava.

It is filled with thousands of tiny holes.

Answers: 1.Amber 2.Open-cast mine 3.Nautilus 4.A hotel in Bolivia 5.Sapphire 6.Platinum 7.The Chauvet Cave, France 8.The Giant's Causeway, Northern Ireland 9.Jade 10.Barite 11.Pumice

47

A safe path

Cave systems can stretch for a long way. Find a safe route out of the underground cave by answering each question correctly.

black

white

red

Cave painters used chalk to create the color...
See page 33

underground fields

Cracks in rocks widen to become...
See page 18

faults

caves

over thousands of years

pearls

Precious stones may be found deep underground, including...
See page 27

diamonds

amber

Do not wander around caves without a parent or known adult.

48

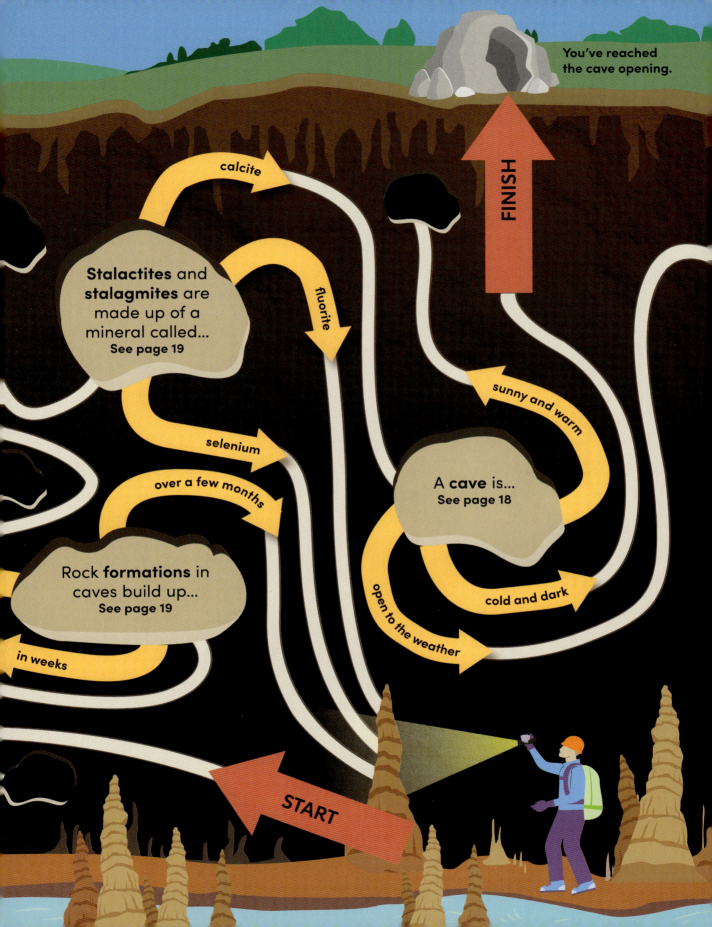

Facts match

Rocks and minerals are found everywhere. Read the clues and see if you can match them with the correct images.

1 We use this white **crystalline rock** almost every day.

2 **Thousands of years ago**, early humans made paintings on cave walls with this.

Peridot

Marble sculpture

Coelacanth

Salt

Meteorite

Sand

Diamond

7 **One of the oldest stones used by humans**, this was shaped and sharpened by chipping at it with a stone.

8 **Some people believe** that this gemstone brings luck to those born in August.

9 This spectacular **rock formation** is made up of soft sandstone. It has a protective cap.

4
This gem is the hardest known mineral.

6
The bright blue color in this metamorphic rock comes from a mineral called lazurite.

3
This sea creature is also called a living fossil.

5
In the Middle Ages, this mineral was commonly used in art.

Pearls

Flint

Hoodoo

Charcoal

Cinnabar

Lapis lazuli

11
This is a chunk from an asteroid that survived a landing on Earth.

13
This precious gem is found inside a living organism. It is commonly used in jewelry.

10
Rocks erode over millions of years to form this sediment.

12
Statues can be carved out of this stone.

Answers: 1.Salt 2.Charcoal 3.Coelacanth 4.Diamond 5.Cinnabar 6.Lapis lazuli 7.Flint 8.Peridot 9.Hoodoo 10.Sand 11.Meteorite 12.Marble 13.Pearl

51

Hunt that treasure!

Rumors tell of a hidden treasure, brimming with precious gems. Will you find it before somebody else beats you to it? Good luck!

What's that glinting near that hoodoo? You've just caught sight of the treasure. **Run three spaces.**

Shelter from a meteorite shower. **Miss a turn.**

Walk past the stalactites and come into the open. **Move ahead by a space.**

Dive into the cave. **Move two spaces.**

Start

Start climbing this cliff to get to the top. **Move one space.**

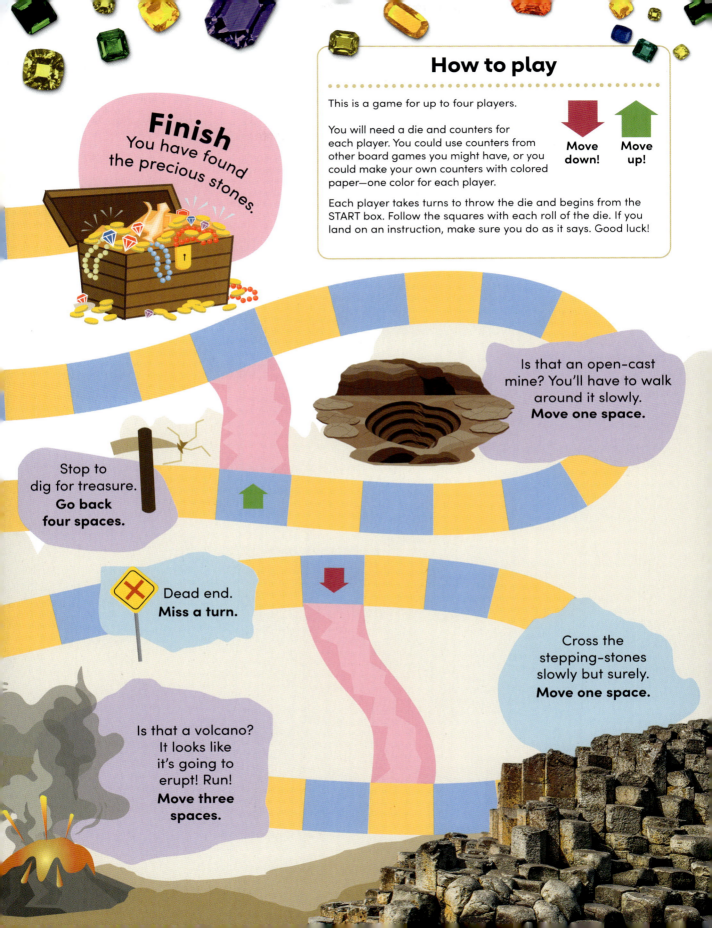

Glossary

Here are the meanings of some words that are useful to know when learning about rocks and minerals.

Acid rain Rainwater polluted by rock-dissolving chemicals.

Alloy A substance that is made from combining two or more metals.

Basalt One of the most common forms of volcanic igneous rock.

Coal A rock made from plants that have been buried and squeezed over millions of years.

Crystal A naturally occurring substance with a specific makeup and structure that forms a mineral.

Erosion The wearing away of Earth's surface features.

Fossil The preserved remains of ancient life or evidence of their activity.

Glacier A mass of ice or snow that flows under its own weight.

Igneous rock Rock made from molten rock that has cooled and hardened.

Hoodoo A column of soft rock with a harder lid that protects it from erosion.

Lava The molten rock (magma) that has erupted from a volcano.

Lignite A woody kind of rock made from plants before they become coal.

Magma Molten rock formed by heat within Earth.

Mantle The part of Earth's interior that lies between the crust and the outer core.

Metamorphic rock Rock changed in form and composition by heat and pressure inside Earth.

Meteor A lump of rock or metal from outer space that burns up as it enters Earth's atmosphere.

Meteorite A meteor that has fallen to Earth.

Mineral A naturally occurring substance with specific characteristics, such as chemical composition.

Nugget A small piece of something valuable, such as gold.

Open-cast mine A mine with an open top instead of tunnels dug under Earth's surface.

Ore A rock with valuable minerals.

Quarry A place where stone is dug up.

Sediment Pieces of rock and plant and animal material that are carried by water, wind, or ice and usually deposited some distance from their origin.

Sedimentary rock Rock formed when small pieces of rock or plant and animal remains stick together over a long period of time.

Weathering The breakdown of rock by the weather.

Index

AB
alloy 31
amethyst 26, 43
ammonite 39, 42, 43
asteroids 16
birthstones 26–27
bricks 36
bronze 31
buildings 11, 36–37

CDE
calcite 18, 19, 42
caves 18–19, 32
chalk 12–13, 33
clay 33, 36, 44
cliffs 8–9, 12
coal 12–13
comet 16, 17
concrete 37
copper 31
crystals 5, 10, 24–25, 43
diamond 27, 43
Earth 4–5, 6, 9
erosion 21

FGH
flint 34, 35
fluorite 42, 44
fossils 27, 39, 40–41, 42–43
fulgurite 39
gems 26–27
Giant's Causeway 10–11
glaciers 22–23
glass 10, 37
gold 28
Grand Canyon 21
granite 5, 11, 34, 38
hoodoos 20–21

IJL
igneous rock 9, 10–11
jade 25
lapis lazuli 15
lava 9, 10, 19, 37
lightning 39
limestone 12–13, 15, 18, 44
lithium 45

MO
magma 6, 8, 15
magnetite 39
marble 15, 26
metals 16, 28–31
metamorphic rock 8, 14–15
meteorite 16, 17
migmatite 14
minerals 4, 5, 30, 38
  in art 32–33
mining 15, 30
Mohs scale 42–43
obsidian 10
ore 30

PQ
Pele's hair 10
platinum 29
pollution 21
pumice 10
quartz 11, 24, 28, 43, 45

RS
rock flour 23
salt 25
sand 13, 24, 37, 39
sediment 9, 13, 40
sedimentary rock 9, 12–13, 18, 33, 40
silver 29, 45
slate 9, 15
sodium 45
space 16–17
stalactites 18
stalagmites 18, 19
sulfur 45

TVW
tools 34–35
volcanoes 6–7, 10
weathering 21

Acknowledgments

The publisher would like to thank the following people for their help with making the book: Andrea Mills for writing text, Steve Hoffman for factchecking, Upamanyu Das and Shahid Qureshi for editorial assistance, and Carron Brown for proofreading and indexing.

The publisher would like to thank the following for their kind permission to reproduce their photographs:

(Key: a-above; b-below/bottom; c-center; f-far; l-left; r-right; t-top)

123RF.com: andreahast 42–43t, 46c, Corey A Ford 43cl, 50c, faabi 12–13, Thomas Hecker 45cr, prapan Ngawkeaw 48–49 (Background), Laurent Renault 27cr, 51cla (Pearl), solarseven 17bc, Anton Starikov 44cb, Tetiana Stupak 4br, 45c, Sujono Sujono / jihane123 52c, Sara Winter 25cla; **Adobe Stock:** ExQuisine 34tc, Yingko 39tr; **Alamy Stock Photo:** Addictive Stock Creatives 14–15b, AGAMI Photo Agency / Sergio Pitamitz 18–19bg, AGF Srl / Antonio Capone 33tr, blickwinkel / Dolder 35cr, Matteo Chinellato 37cra, ColsTravel 25crb, 46bl, Ashley Cooper pics 22–23bc, True Images 43tc, José María Barres Manuel 41clb, Marie-Louise Avery 7clb, Vincent Lowe 23cra, Westend61 GmbH / Biederbick&Rumpf 19crb, Adrian Weston 8–9b, Paul Mayall Australia 17tl, Ryan McGinnis 21cra, The Natural History Museum 12tl, 16clb, News Images LTD / Richard Washbrooke 29br, 47tl, Pillyphotos 44crb, PjrStudio 3tr, 27cb, 46tr, royalty free Arctos photos 51cr, Tillman Schlageter 38–39b, Science Photo Library / Mark Garlick 5tr, Rosanne Tackaberry 23cr, Robin Weaver 23cra, Westend61 GmbH / Biederbick&Rumpf 19crb, Adrian Weston 8–9b, World History Archive 33bl; **Depositphotos Inc:** anatchant@gmail.com 26br, AntonMatyukha 51cr (Charcoal), ChinaImages 54–55, Redpixel 45c (Camera); **Dorling Kindersley:** Colin Keates / Natural History Museum 10tl, Harry Taylor / Natural History Museum, London 10cla, Holts Gems / Gary Ombler 43bc, Holts Gems / Ruth Jenkinson 24–25t, 26bl (Amethyst), 26bc, 26bc (Garnet), 26br (Emerald), 45tl, Holts Gems, Hatton Garden / Richard Leeney 27bc (Sapphire), Natural History Museum / Tim Parmenter 26cb, 43br (diamond), Natural History Museum, London 51cc, Natural History Museum, London / Colin Keates 5clb, 7cb, 7crb, 25tc, 27bc, 29clb, 39tl, 40l, Natural History Museum, London / Frank Greenaway 18–19t, Natural History Museum, London / Tim Parmenter 27br, Oxford University Museum of Natural / Gary Ombler 43br, Oxford University Museum of Natural History 50cr, RGB Research Limited / Ruth Jenkinson 45cla, 45bl, Science Museum, Londo / Dave King 45br, Science Museum, London / Dave King 35br; **Dreamstime.com:** Abel Tumik / Yamahavalerossi 45bc (Indigo), Ferli Achirulli Kamaruddin 44bc, Alexan24 37ca, Alisali 33br, Andreadonetti 15cb, Andreykuzmin 37cra (glass), Annegordon 7bc, Mohammed Anwarul Kabir Choudhury 13bc, Anton Arlansyah 43c, Artrecphotography 25cl, Bartkowski 10–11b, 47cl, Belish 16tr, Bennymarty 22–23t, Boborsillo 41br, Choneschones 50cra, Cosmin Constantin Sava 45cb, Czuber 36ca, 44cla, Elilarionova 11tr, Empire331 44clb, Epitavi 26ca, 46crb, Oksana Ermak 37cla, Fireflyphoto 28cr, Fokinol 5cb, 5crb, Globo360gradi 42br, Goir

50cb, Jakub Gojda 8–9t, Hellem 45c (Matchsticks), Igor Kaliuzhny / Igorkali 50crb, Fabio Iozzino 41cb, Italianestro 37cra (Concrete), Jongcreative 52tr, Jorisvo 17cr, Maksim Karamyshev 5bc, Natalia Kazarina 44cl, Rob Kemp 10–11ca, 47crb, Kewuwu 44cra, Tetiana Kovalenko 32bc, KPixMining 31tr, Laindiapiaroa 13tr, Michele Lombardo 8–9c, Oleksii Lukin 13tl, Marcovarro 31l, Saskia Massink 45ca (Dentures), Micropic 26clb, Ruslan Minakryn 43bl (Apatite), Moviephotoo 45tc (clock), Juan Moyano 44c, Christian Mueringer 5br, Thaweesak Nammaneewong 53cra, Noiral 26–27t, Kevin Oke 19tr, Mohamed Osama 45bc, Sean Pavone 7t, Prostockstudio 42bc, Rjmiguel 45cr (desert), Elena Schweitzer 45crb, Sever180 44br, Natdanai Siammai 36cla, Solarseven 16–17b, Anton Starikov 37cla (Sand), Deni Sugandi 6tr, Superjoseph 20cla, Winai Tepsuttinun 45cra, Evgeny Tkachev 13cr, Toscawhi 27bl, 51cla, Tropper2000 44ca (pencil), Tuja66 13br, Tycoon751 33clb, Cenk Unver / Zensu 15br, Viovita 13bl, Vovaanty 13bl, Vvoevale 27crb, 31cr, 45bl, Krystyna Wojciechowska Czarnik 39cla, 47bl, Bj'rn Wylezich 29cra, 31cra, 39cr, 45cl, 51cb; **French Ministry of Culture and Communication, Regional Direction for Cultural Affairs—Rhône-Alpes region—Regional department of archaeology:** J. Clottes / MC 32c, 47tr; **Getty Images:** AFP / Carl De Souza 41cra, Moment / kampee patisena 52–53t; **Getty Images / iStock:** Caroline Brundle Bugge 3br, 34–35b, Liudmila Chernetska 44cr, CostinT 4bc, 45tc, E+ / ASMR 36–37b, E+ / gremlin 5bl, Gannet77 44ca, 44bc (Books), pashapixel 45tr; **The Metropolitan Museum of Art:** Gift and Bequest of Alice K. Bache, 1974, 1977 29cla, Gift of Heber R. Bishop, 1902 25b, 47cr, Gift of J. Pierpont Morgan, 1905 29tr (X2), Rogers Fund, 1911 50cl; **Science Photo Library:** Doug Martin 2br, 43cr, David Nunuk 20–21b; **Shutterstock.com:** Marti Bug Catcher 53br, EmEvn 36cra, HERREROS 30–31t, 46cl, Sebastian Janicki 1, 14–15t, Joel_420 45ca, Yes058 Montree Nanta 15cra, richchy 28l, RobSt 30crb, Albert Russ 26crb; **Unsplash:** Sonaal Bangera 21tl.

Cover images: Front: **123RF.com:** andreahast crb; **Adobe Stock:** Sebastian tr/ (Lapis); **Alamy Stock Photo:** Matteo Chinellato bl/ (Libyan); **Dorling Kindersley:** Harry Taylor / Natural History Museum, London tl, Holts Gems / Ruth Jenkinson clb, cb, cb/ (Emerald), bl, Ruth Jenkinson / Holts Gems c/ (Citrine), Richard Leeney / Holts Gems c/ (Tourmaline), Natural History Museum, London / Colin Keates ca, Oxford University Museum of Natural History / Gary Ombler cla/ (Calcite); **Dreamstime.com:** Anetlanda tc, Bwylezich crb/ (Crystalline), Globo360gradi bc, Hapelena crb/ (Vanadinite), Joools cla, Daniel Nagy br, Noiral cra/ (Diamond), Vvoevale tr; **The Metropolitan Museum of Art:** Purchase, Joseph Pulitzer Bequest, 1966 clb/ (Bull); **Science Photo Library:** Dirk Wiersma c; **Shutterstock.com:** NTV cr; Back: **Dorling Kindersley:** Ruth Jenkinson / Holts Gems cla/ (Gem), Natural History Museum, London / Colin Keates tc, tr, tl/ (Gold), clb, br, bl, Oxford University Museum of Natural History / Gary Ombler cra; **Dreamstime.com:** Annausova75 cl, Anat Chantrakool cr, KPixMining ca, Ruslan Minakryn bc, Valentyn75 tl, Vlad3563 cla.